Novels for Students, Volume 2

Since this page cannot legibly accommodate all copyright notices, the acknowledgments constitute an extension of the copyright notice.

While every effort has been made to secure permission to reprint material and to ensure the reliability of the information presented in this publication, Gale Research neither guarantees the accuracy of the data contained herein nor assumes any responsibility for errors, omissions or discrepancies. Gale accepts no payment for listing; and inclusion in the publication of any organization, agency, institution, publication, service, or individual does not imply endorsement of the editors or publisher. Errors brought to the attention of the publisher and verified to the satisfaction of the publisher will be corrected in future editions.

This publication is a creative work fully protected by all applicable copyright laws, as well as by misappropriation, trade secret, unfair competition, and other applicable laws. The authors and editors of this work have added value to the underlying factual material herein through one or more of the following: unique and original selection, coordination, expression, arrangement, and classification of the information.

All rights to this publication will be vigorously defended.

Copyright © 1997

Gale Research
835 Penobscot Building
645 Griswold St.
Detroit, Ml 48226-4094

This book is printed on acid-free paper that meets the minimum requirements of American National Standard for Information Sciences—Permanence Paper for Printed Library Materials, ANSI Z39.48-1984.

ISBN 0-7876-1687-7
ISSN 1094-3552

Printed in the United States of America
10 9 8 7 6 5 4

To Kill a Mockingbird

Harper Lee

1960

Introduction

When *To Kill a Mockingbird* was published in 1960, it brought its young first-time author, Harper Lee, a startling amount of attention and notoriety. The novel replays three key years in the life of Scout Finch, the young daughter of an Alabama town's principled lawyer. The work was an instant sensation, becoming a best-seller and winning the Pulitzer Prize for fiction. Scout's narrative relates how she and her elder brother Jem learn about fighting prejudice and upholding human dignity through the example of their father. Atticus Finch has taken on the legal defense of a black man who has been falsely charged with raping a white woman. Lee's story of the events surrounding the trial has been admired for its portrayal of Southern life during the 1930s, not only for its piercing examination of the causes and effects of racism, but because it created a model of tolerance and courage in the character of Atticus Finch. Some early reviewers found Scout's narration unconvincing, its style and language too sophisticated for a young girl. Since then, however, critics have hailed Lee's rendering of a child's perspective—as told by an experienced adult—as one of the most technically proficient in modern fiction. A regional novel dealing with universal themes of tolerance, courage, compassion, and justice, *To Kill a Mockingbird* combined popular appeal with literary excellence to ensure itself an enduring place in modern American literature.

Although Harper Lee has long maintained that *To Kill a Mockingbird* is not autobiographical, critics have often remarked upon the striking similarities between the author's own childhood and that of her youthful heroine, Scout Finch. Nelle Harper Lee was born in 1926, the youngest of three children of Amasa Coleman Lee, a lawyer who practiced in the small town of Monroeville, Alabama. Like Scout, who could be bullied into submission with the remark that she was "gettin' more like a girl," Lee was "a rough 'n' tough tomboy," according to childhood friends. Summers in Monroeville were brightened by the visits of young Truman Capote, who stayed with the Lees' next-door neighbors and who later became a famous writer himself. The games young Nelle and her brother played with Capote were likely the inspiration for the adventures Scout and Jem had with Dill, their own "summer" friend.

After graduating from the public schools of Monroeville, Lee attended a small college in nearby Montgomery before attending the University of Alabama for four years. She left school six months short of earning a law degree, however, in order to pursue a writing career. In the early 1950s, the author worked as an airline reservations clerk in New York City, writing essays and short stories in her spare time. After her literary agent suggested that one of her stories might be expanded into a novel, Lee quit her airline job. With the financial support of some friends, she spent several years revising the manuscript of *To Kill a Mockingbird* before submitting it to publishers. Several more months of revision followed the feedback of her editors, who found the original version more like a string of short stories than a cohesive novel. The final draft was finally completed in 1959 and published in 1960. The novel was a dramatic success, earning generally positive reviews and achieving bestseller status. Lee herself attained considerable celebrity as the novel won the Pulitzer Prize for fiction in 1961 and was made into an Oscar-winning film in 1962. Since then, aside from a few magazine pieces in the early 1960s, the reclusive author has published nothing, although she has been reported to have been working on a second novel. Despite the lack of a follow-up work, Lee's literary reputation remains secure and even has grown since the debut of her remarkable first novel.

Part One

Harper Lee's *To Kill a Mockingbird* depicts the life of its young narrator, Jean Louise "Scout" Finch, in the small town of Maycomb, Alabama, in the mid-1930s. Scout opens the novel as a grown woman reflecting back on key events in her childhood. The novel covers a two-year period, beginning when Scout is six and ending when she is eight. She lives with her father, Atticus, a widowed lawyer, and her older brother, Jem (short for Jeremy). Their black housekeeper, Calpurnia, tends to the children. Scout and Jem's summer playmate, Dill Harris, shares the Finch children's adventures and adds imagination and intrigue to their game playing. In the novel, we see Scout grow in awareness and come to new understandings about her town, her family, and herself.

During the summer before Scout enters school, the children become fascinated with Arthur "Boo" Radley, a reclusive neighbor. Radley's father, a religious fanatic, confined Boo to the house because he was arrested for youthful pranks as a teenager. Some years later, Boo casually stabbed his father in the leg with a pair of scissors, confirming people's worst fears about him. The children are naturally afraid of and intrigued by such a "malevolent phantom," as Scout calls him. Yet they only approach the house once, when Jem runs and touches the porch on a dare.

Scout enters first grade the following September and must confront new challenges and learn new ways to deal with people. She cannot understand, for instance, her young teacher's lack of familiarity with the town families and their peculiarities, such as the Cunningham children's poverty and pride. Later, Atticus explains to Scout that she must put herself in others' places before judging them, one of the many lessons she learns by making mistakes.

With summer's return, Dill arrives and the children's absorption with Boo Radley begins again in earnest. Ultimately, they attempt to look in the house to see Boo, but a shotgun blast from Nathan Radley, Boo's brother, drives them off. In their panic, Jem catches his overalls in the Radley fence and must abandon them. Later that night, he returns to retrieve them and finds them neatly folded on the fence with the ripped fabric poorly resewn.

Their contact with Boo Radley continues into the school year. Before the previous summer, Scout and Jem had discovered gum and Indian head pennies in a knotholed tree by the Radley house. Now more objects begin to appear in the knothole, including replicas of Scout and Jem carved in soap. They decide to leave a note for whoever is leaving the objects, but before they can, Nathan Radley fills the hole with cement, upsetting Jem.

Scout soon encounters trouble at school when

a schoolmate condemns Atticus for "defending niggers." Atticus confirms that he is defending a black man named Tom Robinson, who is accused of raping a white woman, and that his conscience compels him to do no less. He warns her that she will encounter more accusations of this kind and to remember that despite their views, the people who cast slurs at them are still their friends. Atticus later tells his brother Jack that he hopes he can guide his children through this time without them becoming bitter and "without catching Maycomb's usual disease" of racism.

That Christmas, Atticus gives the children airrifles and admonishes them to shoot no mockingbirds. Miss Maudie Atkinson, their neighbor, explains Atticus's reasons when she says that "Mockingbirds don't do one thing but make music for us to enjoy." Hence, it is a sin to kill them. At this time, the children feel disappointed in Atticus because he is old (almost fifty) and does nothing of interest. They soon learn, however, about one of their father's unique talents when he shoots a rabid dog that threatens the neighborhood, killing the beast with one shot. The neighbors tell them that Atticus is the best shot in the county, he just chooses not to shoot a gun unless he must. Scout admires Atticus for his shooting talent, but Jem admires him for his gentlemanly restraint.

Part Two

The family's involvement in Tom Robinson's

trial dominates Part Two of the novel. One personal inconvenience of the trial is the arrival of Aunt Alexandra, Atticus's sister, who comes to tend to the family. Scout finds her presence unwelcome because Aunt Alexandra disapproves of her tomboyish dress and activities and tries to make Scout wear dresses and attend women's socials.

The time for the trial arrives, and Atticus guards the jail door the night Tom Robinson is brought to Maycomb. The children, including Dill, sneak out to watch over him and soon become involved in a standoff. Carloads of men drive up and demand that Atticus let them have Tom Robinson, and he gently refuses. Scout recognizes a schoolmate's father, Mr. Cunningham, and asks him polite questions about his legal debt to Atticus, who did work for him, and about his son. Scout's innocent questioning of Mr. Cunningham shames him, and he convinces the men to leave.

The children also sneak to the courthouse to attend the trial. They sit in the balcony with the black townspeople because no seats are available on the ground floor. Atticus's questioning of Bob Ewell and Mayella Ewell, both of whom claim Tom Robinson beat and raped Mayella, reveals their lies. Mayella was beaten primarily on the right side of her body by a lefthanded man. By having Bob Ewell sign his name, Atticus shows him to be lefthanded. Tom Robinson's left arm, however, is crippled from a boyhood accident. Tom's story rings truer. He contends that Mayella invited him into the house and tried to seduce him, a story made credible by Mayella's and Tom's descriptions of her lonely life. Tom resisted her advances, but before he could leave Bob Ewell discovered them. Tom ran and Ewell beat Mayella. To avoid social disgrace, the Ewells claimed Tom had raped her.

Despite the evidence, Tom is convicted. Atticus has expected this verdict and believes he can win on appeal. Jem has difficulty accepting the injustice of the verdict. Others, however, remain angry over Atticus's sincere defense of Robinson, particularly Bob Ewell. Ewell confronts Atticus, threatens him, and spits on him. Soon after, Tom Robinson's story ends in tragedy as he is shot trying to escape from prison. He ran because he believed he could find no justice in a whitedominated legal system.

The following October, Scout dresses as a ham for the school Halloween pageant. On the way home from the pageant, she and Jem are followed, then attacked. Scout cannot see their assailant because of her costume, but she hears Jem grappling with him and hears Jem being injured. After the confused struggle, she feels a man lying on the ground and sees another man carrying Jem. She follows them home. The doctor arrives and assures her that Jem is alive and has suffered only a broken arm. The man who carried him home is standing in Jem's room. To Scout's tearful amazement, she realizes that he is Boo Radley. Sheriff Heck Tate informs them that Bob Ewell attacked them and that only Scout's costume saved her. Ewell himself now lies dead, stabbed in the ribs. Atticus believes Jem killed

Ewell in self-defense, but Tate makes him realize that Boo Radley actually stabbed Ewell and saved both children's lives. The men agree to claim that Ewell fell on his knife in order to save Boo the spectacle of a trial. Scout walks Boo home:

> He had to stoop a little to accommodate me, but if Miss Stephanie Crawford was watching from her upstairs window, she would see Arthur Radley escorting me down the sidewalk, as any gentleman would do.
>
> We came to the street light on the corner, and I wondered how many times Dill had stood there hugging the fat pole, watching, waiting, hoping. I wondered how many times Jem and I had made this journey, but I entered the Radley front gate for the second time in my life. Boo and I walked up the steps to the porch. His fingers found the front doorknob. He gently released my hand, opened the door, went inside, and shut the door behind him. I never saw him again.
>
> Neighbors bring food with death and flowers with sickness and little things in between. Boo was our neighbor. He gave us two soap dolls, a broken watch and chain, a pair of good-luck pennies, and our lives. But neighbors give in return. We never

put back into the tree what we took
out of it; we had given him nothing,
and it made me sad.

She returns home to Atticus, who stays up all
night waiting for Jem to awake.

Characters

Aunt Alexandra

See Alexandra Finch Hancock

Miss Maudie Atkinson

Maudie Atkinson is a strong, supportive woman who lives across the street from the Finches. A forthright speaker, she never condescends to Jem and Scout, but speaks to them as equals. It is Miss Maudie who affirms that it is a sin to kill a mockingbird, since "they don't do one thing but sing their hearts out for us." A respected community member who often teasingly reproaches the children, Miss Maudie nevertheless has a impish streak: she likes to quote scripture back to conservative religious folk who frown on her brightly colored garden. Miss Maudie provides another example of bravery to the children when her home bums down. Instead of lamenting her fate, she tells Jem she looks forward to rebuilding a smaller house which will have more room for her flowers.

Mr. Avery

A good-natured if somewhat coarse neighbor of the Finches who helps fight the fire at Miss Maudie's house at risk to his own life.

Calpurnia

One of several strong female figures in the lives of the Finch children, Calpurnia is the family's black housekeeper. She has helped to raise Jem and Scout since their mother's death four years ago. Like Atticus, Calpurnia is a strict but loving teacher, particularly in regard to Scout, whose enthusiasm sometimes makes her thoughtless. On Scout's first day of school, for example, Calpurnia scolds Scout for criticizing the table manners of Walter Cunningham Jr., whom the children have brought home as a lunch guest. That day after school, however, Calpurnia prepares Scout's favorite food, crackling bread, as a special treat. Calpurnia also gives Scout her first awareness of the contrast between the worlds of black and white. During a visit to Calpurnia's church, her use of black dialect with her friends makes Scout realize that Calpurnia has a wider life outside the Finch household. Calpurnia also helps Scout understand how people can serve as a bridge between these differing worlds. Although the majority of parishioners welcome them during their church visit, one woman challenges the white children. Calpurnia responds by calling them her guests and saying "it's the same God, ain't it?"

Stephanie Crawford

The "neighborhood scold" who is always ready to gossip about anything or anyone.

Walter Cunningham Jr.

A poor but proud classmate of Scout's.

Walter Cunningham Sr.

Walter Cunningham, Sr., is a member of a poor family who "never took anything they couldn't pay back." A former client of Atticus's, he paid for legal service with goods such as firewood and hickory nuts. After Scout recognizes him in the potential lynch mob and speaks to him of his son, he leads the crowd away from violence.

Link Deas

A local farmer who hires a lot of black help and once employed Tom Robinson.

Mrs. Henry Lafayette Dubose

According to Scout, Mrs. Henry Lafayette Dubose is "the meanest old woman who ever lived." She regularly insults and harasses the children as they walk by. When Jem wrecks her garden in retaliation for a nasty remark about his father, Atticus punishes him by forcing him to spend many hours reading to her. She dies later that year, and Jem learns that his reading helped her to courageously defeat an addiction to morphine.

Bob Ewell

The head of family who's been "the disgrace of Maycomb for three generations," Bob Ewell is despised by Maycomb society as a shiftless drunkard. He is unable to keep a job, spends all his relief money on alcohol, and traps animals outside of hunting season. He provides little support to his large, motherless family, and is reputed to beat his children (and perhaps sexually abuse them too, as Mayella's testimony hints). Angered and shamed by his exposure on the witness stand, Ewell makes threats to Atticus and others involved in the trial, but never risks direct confrontation. This cowardice reaches its peak in his violent attack on Scout and Jem, during which he is killed by Boo Radley.

Mayella Ewell

The eldest daughter of Bob Ewell, Mayella Ewell lives a lonely life keeping house for her father and seven siblings without assistance. Although she can only afford small gestures such as a potted plant, Mayella tries to brighten her situation and the lives of her siblings. During the trial it is revealed that Tom Robinson's occasional stops to help her with heavy chores were her only contact with a sympathetic soul. When Bob Ewell discovers Mayella's attempt to seduce the unwilling Tom, his violent outburst leads her to accuse Tom of rape. Despite her situation, she loses the reader's sympathy when she repays Tom's kindness with open contempt and a lie that costs him his life. The fact that the jury accepts her word over his, even when it is demonstrated to be false, further illustrates the malicious power of racist thinking.

Mrs. Gertrude Farrow

One of the hypocritical members of Aunt Alexandra's missionary circle.

Atticus Finch

Atticus Finch, Scout's widowed father, is a member of one of Maycomb County's oldest and most prominent families. Nevertheless, he refuses to use his background as an excuse to hold himself above others and instead is a model of tolerance and understanding. Atticus is a lawyer and also a member of the state legislature, elected by townspeople who respect his honesty even if they don't always approve of his actions. For example, when Atticus is appointed the defense attorney for Tom Robinson, a black man accused of raping a white woman, the town disapproves because he aims to do the best job he can. As a father Atticus is affectionate with Jem and Scout, ready with a hug when they need comfort and available to spend time reading to them. Although he allows his children freedom to play and explore, he is also a firm disciplinarian, always teaching his children to think of how their actions affect others and devising punishments to teach his children valuable lessons. When Jem damages the camellia bushes of Mrs. Henry Lafayette Dubose, a neighbor who scolds and insults the children, Atticus sentences him to read to her each day. As Jem reads, he and Scout witness the dying woman's battle against her morphine addiction and learn the true meaning of courage: "it's when you know you're licked before you begin but you see it through no matter what," Atticus tells them. Atticus's own actions in arguing the Robinson case demonstrate this kind of courage, and his behavior throughout embodies values of dignity, integrity, determination, and tolerance. Although Atticus's character is somewhat idealized, critic William T. Going calls Lee's creation "the most memorable portrait in recent fiction of the just and equitable Southern liberal."

Jack Finch

See John Hale Finch

Jean Louise Finch

The narrator of the novel, Jean Louise "Scout" Finch is almost six years old at the time her story begins. A tomboy most frequently clad in overalls, Scout spends much of her time with her older brother Jem and is constantly trying to prove herself his equal. Throughout the book Scout maintains an innocence and an innate sense of right and wrong that makes her the ideal observer of events, even if she doesn't always fully understand them. She naturally questions the injustices she sees instead of accepting them as "the way things are." For instance, she doesn't understand why her aunt makes social distinctions based on "background" when Scout thinks "there's just one kind of folks:

Folks." Her independence and outspokenness often get Scout into trouble, however; she is quick to respond to insults with her fists and frequently opens her mouth at inappropriate moments, as when she rudely remarks on the table manners of a guest. By the end of the novel, however, eight-year-old Scout has learned a measure of restraint, primarily through the influence and example of her father Atticus.

Jem Finch

See Jeremy Finch

Media Adaptations

- To Kill a Mockingbird was adapted as a film by Horton Foote, starring Gregory Peck and Mary Badham, Universal, 1962; available from MCA/Universal Home Video.

- It was also adapted as a full-length stage play by Christopher Sergel, and was published as *Harper Lee's To Kill a Mockingbird: A Fulllength Play,* Dramatic Publishing Co., 1970.

Jeremy Finch

Four years older than his sister Scout, Jeremy "Jem" Finch seems to have a deeper understanding of the events during the three years of the novel, for his emotional reactions to them are stronger. As the story begins, Jem is a quick-witted but funloving ten year old who spends a lot of time in creative play with Scout and Dill Harris, a summer visitor to the neighborhood. Jem is frequently exasperated by his sister, and requires her to keep her distance during school hours. Nevertheless, for the most part Jem is an understanding and encouraging older brother, allowing Scout to join in his games and even dignifying her with an occasional fistfight. He is anxious to please his father, and hates to disappoint him. When Jem loses his pants in the "raid" on the Radley house, he insists on returning for them during the middle of the night—not so much to avoid the pain of punishment, but because "Atticus ain't ever whipped me since I can remember. I wanta keep it that way." As he approaches adolescence, however, Jem becomes quieter and more easily agitated: he reacts angrily when Mrs. Dubose leaves him a small peace offering after her death. Although more socially aware than Scout, he is genuinely surprised at Tom Robinson's guilty verdict. The trial leaves Jem a little more withdrawn and less self-confident, and he spends much of the following fall concerned for his father's safety. He demonstrates his own courage, however, when he protects his sister from the attack of Bob Ewell without regard for his own safety.

John Hale Finch

Atticus's younger brother, a doctor who left Maycomb to study in Boston.

Scout Finch

See Jean Louise Finch

Miss Caroline Fisher

Scout's first-grade teacher who is a newcomer to Maycomb. She misunderstands the social order of Maycomb and punishes Scout for trying to explain it. She also comes into conflict with Scout because of the girl's reading ability.

Miss Gates

Scout's hypocritical third-grade teacher who condemns Hitler's persecution of the Jews even as she discriminates against her own students and complains about blacks "getting above themselves."

Mr. Gilmer

The circuit prosecutor from Abbottsville who leads the case against Tom Robinson.

Alexandra Finch Hancock

Atticus's sister, Alexandra Finch Hancock, is a conservative woman concerned with social and class distinctions and bound to the traditions of the South. She tries to counteract her brother's liberal influence on his children by reminding them of their family's eminence and by trying to make Scout behave in a more ladylike manner. When she moves in with Atticus's family, her efforts to reform Scout include requiring her attendance at regular meetings of a "missionary circle," whose discussions focus on improving the lives of "heathens" in distant Africa rather than on the needy in their own town. Aunt Alexandra is not completely unsympathetic, however; she also shows—in private—some anger towards the hypocrites in her missionary circle. Although she disapproves of Atticus's role in the Robinson case, she becomes upset upon hearing news of Robinson's death during one of her parties. Her ability to continue on leads Scout to state that "if Auntie could be a lady at a time like this, so could I."

Francis Hancock

Scout and Jem's cousin and Alexandra's grandson.

Charles Baker Harris

Small and devilish, Charles Baker "Dill" Harris is Scout and Jem's summer friend. He instigates much of the children's mischief by daring Jem to perform acts such as approaching the Radley house. He seems to have a limitless imagination, and his appeal is only enhanced by his firsthand knowledge of movies such as *Dracula*. Seemingly ignored (but not neglected) by his parents, Dill enjoys his yearly visits to his aunt, Rachel Haverford, who lives next door to the Finches—he even runs away from home one summer to come to Maycomb. A year older than Scout, Dill has declared he will one day marry her, a statement she seems to accept matter-offactly.

Dill Harris

See Charles Baker Harris

Rachel Haverford

Dill Harris's sympathetic aunt, who lives next door to the Finches.

Grace Merriweather

A member of Alexandra's missionary circle who has a reputation as the "most devout lady in Maycomb" even though she is a hypocritical bigot.

Arthur Radley

Arthur "Boo" Radley has a strong presence in the novel even though he isn't seen until its last pages. A local legend for several years, Boo is rumored to wander the neighborhood at night and dine on raw squirrels and cats. He has spent the last fifteen years secluded in his own house. An adolescent prank led his late father to place him under house arrest. His sinister reputation stems from a later incident, when it was rumored that he stabbed his father in the leg with a pair of scissors. Boo becomes a central figure in the imaginations of Scout, Jem, and their neighbor Dill Harris, for their summers are occupied with dramatic re-creations of his life and plans to lure "the monster" out of his house. Despite his history of being abused by his father, Boo is revealed to be a gentle soul through his unseen acts: the gifts he leaves in the tree; his mending of Jem's torn pants; the blanket he puts around Scout the night of the fire; and finally, his rescue of the children from Bob Ewell's murderous attack. The children's fear of Boo Radley, based on ignorance rather than knowledge, subtly reflects the prejudice of the town against Tom Robinson—a connection mirrored in the use of mockingbird imagery for both men.

Boo Radley

See Arthur Radley

Nathan Radley

Boo's hardhearted older brother who spoils Boo's secret game with the children by filling the empty treehole with cement.

Dolphus Raymond

A local man from a good white family with property who has a black mistress and children. He fosters a reputation as a drunk to give townspeople a reason to excuse his flaunting of social taboos.

Tom Robinson

Tom Robinson is a mild-mannered, conscientious black man whose kind acts earn him only trouble when Mayella Ewell accuses him of rape. Because he saw she was left alone to maintain the household without any help from her family, he often performed small chores for her. During his testimony, he relates that he felt sorry for the girl. This remark affronts the white men in the jury, who see it as evidence that he is overreaching his social station. Although he is clearly proven innocent, the all-white jury convicts him of rape, a crime punishable by death. Unconvinced that he can find justice on appeal, Robinson attempts to escape from his prison camp and is shot dead.

Reverend Sykes

The minister of Maycomb's black church.

Heck Tate

The sheriff of Maycomb who is sympathetic towards Atticus and who insists on keeping Boo Radley's role in the death of Bob Ewell a secret.

Judge John Taylor

The deceivingly sleepy but fair judge whose sympathy for Tom Robinson can be seen in the fact that he appointed Atticus, whom he knew would do his best, as Robinson's public defender.

Uncle Jack

See John Hale Finch

B. B. Underwood

See Braxton Bragg Underwood

Braxton Bragg Underwood

The owner and editor of the local newspaper who was ready to defend Atticus and Tom Robinson from the lynch mob with a shotgun even though he is known to "despise" black people.

Themes

Prejudice and Tolerance

Comprising the main portion of the book's examination of racism and its effects are the underlying themes of prejudice vs. tolerance: how people feel about and respond to differences in others. At one end of the spectrum are people who fear and hate, such as the members of the jury who convict an innocent man of rape because of his race. Atticus and Calpurnia, on the other hand, show understanding and sympathy towards those who might be different or less fortunate. When Scout brings a poor classmate home for dinner and then belittles his table manners, for instance, Calpurnia scolds her for remarking upon them and tells her she is bound to treat all guests with respect no matter what their social station. Atticus similarly bases his opinions of people on their behavior and not their background. Unlike Alexandra, who calls poor people like the Cunninghams "trash" because of their social station, Atticus tells his children that any white man who takes advantage of a black man's ignorance is "trash."

Guilt and Innocence

Closely linked to these themes of prejudice are issues of guilt and innocence, for the same ignorance that creates racist beliefs underlies assumptions of guilt. The most obvious instance is the case of Tom Robinson: the jury's willingness to believe what Atticus calls "the evil assumption ... that *all* Negroes are basically immoral beings" leads them to convict an innocent man. Boo Radley, unknown by a community who has not seen or heard from him in fifteen years, is similarly presumed to be a monster by the court of public opinion. Scout underscores this point when she tells her Uncle Jack he has been unfair in assigning all the blame to her after her fight with Cousin Francis. If he had stopped to learn both sides of the situation he might have judged her differently—which he eventually does. The novel's conclusion also reinforces the theme of guilt and innocence, as Atticus reads Scout a book about a boy falsely accused of vandalism. As Scout summarizes: "When they finally saw him, why he hadn't done any of those things. Atticus, he was real nice." To which Atticus responds, "Most people are, once you see them."

Knowledge and Ignorance

Because a lack of understanding leads to prejudice and false assumptions of guilt, themes of ignorance and knowledge also play a large role in the novel. Lee seems to suggest that children have a natural instinct for tolerance and understanding; only as they grow older do they learn to react to differences with fear and disdain. For example, Scout is confused when one of Dolphus Raymond's mixedrace children is pointed out to her. The child looks "all Negro" to Scout, who wonders why it matters that "you just hafta know who [the mixedrace children] are." That same day Dill is made sick during the trial by the way in which Mr. Gilmer, the prosecuting attorney, sneeringly crossexamines Tom Robinson. As Dolphus Raymond tells Scout, "Things haven't caught up with that one's instinct yet. Let him get a little older and he won't get sick and cry." Lee seems to imply that children learn important lessons about life through the examples of others, not through school. In an ironic commentary on the nature of knowledge, formal education—as Scout experiences it—fails to teach or even contradicts these important lessons. Scout's first-grade teacher, Miss Caroline Fisher, is more concerned with making her students follow a system than in teaching them as individuals. This is why she forbids Scout to continue reading with her father, whose "unqualified" instruction would "interfere" with her education. Whatever the method, however, the most important factor in gaining knowledge is an individual's motivation. As Calpurnia tells Scout, people "got to want to learn themselves, and when they don't want to learn there's nothing you can do but keep your mouth shut or learn their language."

Topics for Further Study

- Research the 1930s trials of the Scottsboro Boys and compare how the justice system worked in this case to the trial of Tom Robinson.

- Explore the government programs of President Franklin D. Roosevelt's "New Deal" and explain how some of the characters in *To Kill a Mockingbird* could have been helped by them.

- Investigate the various groups involved in the Civil Rights Movement of the 1950s and 1960s and compare their programs to the community supports found in Lee's imaginary town of Maycomb.

Courage and Cowardice

Another important theme appearing throughout the novel is that of cowardice and heroism, for Scout observes several different kinds of courage during her childhood. The most common definition of bravery is being strong in the face of physical danger. Atticus demonstrates this when he stops in the path of a rabid dog and drops it with one rifle shot. Other kinds of courage, however, rely more on moral fortitude. For instance, Atticus talks pleasantly to Mrs. Henry Lafayette Dubose, even though she regularly heaps verbal abuse on him and his children. At times like these, Scout says, she thought "my father, who hated guns and had never been to any wars, was the bravest man who ever lived." Mrs. Dubose teaches the children another lesson in courage when Jem is sentenced to spend two hours a day reading to her as repayment for the flowers he damaged. Scout tags along as Jem visits after school to read Sir Walter Scott's *Ivanhoe,* a tale of chivalry and heroism. Mrs. Dubose's behavior seems strange; she often drifts off during the readings and begins to drool and have seizures. After her death some months later, the children discover that she was trying to overcome an addiction to morphine, a painkiller. Jem's reading served as a distraction that helped her die free from addiction. Atticus tells his children that despite her faults, Mrs. Dubose was the bravest person he ever knew, for real courage is "when you know you're licked before you begin but you begin anyway and you see it through no matter what." Atticus shows the same type of bravery in fighting the Robinson case; although he knows it would be nearly impossible for a white jury to return a verdict of "not guilty," he nonetheless argues the case to the best of his ability. In contrast to Atticus's bravery stands the cowardly behavior of Bob Ewell, who never directly faces those whom he thinks have wronged him. He vandalizes Judge Taylor's home when he thinks no one is there; he throws rocks and harasses Helen Robinson, Tom's widow, from a distance; and assaults Atticus's children as they walk alone on a deserted street at night.

Point of View

The most outstanding aspect of *To Kill a Mockingbird's* construction lies in its distinctive narrative point of view. Scout Finch, who narrates in the first person ("I"), is nearly six years old when the novel opens. The story, however, is recalled by the adult Scout; this allows her first-person narrative to contain adult language and adult insights yet still maintain the innocent outlook of a child. The adult perspective also adds a measure of hindsight to the tale, allowing for a deeper examination of events. The narrative proceeds in a straightforward and linear fashion, only jumping in time when relating past events as background to some present occurrence. Scout's account is broken into two parts: the two years before the trial, and the summer of the trial and the autumn that follows. Some critics have proposed that Part II itself should have been broken into two parts, the trial and the Halloween pageant; William T. Going suggests that this arrangement would keep the latter section from "seeming altogether an anticlimax to the trial of Tom."

Setting

The setting of *To Kill a Mockingbird* is another big factor in the story, for the action never leaves the town of Maycomb, Alabama. Maycomb is described variously as "an old town," "an ancient town," and "a tired old town," suggesting a conservative place that is steeped in tradition and convention. Scout's description of the local courthouse reinforces this impression. The building combines large Greek-style pillars—the only remnants from the original building that burned years ago—with the early Victorian design of its replacement. The result is an architectural oddity that indicates "a people determined to preserve every physical scrap of the past." The time of the novel is also significant, for the years 1933 to 1935 were in the midst of the Great Depression. These economic hard times affected the entire town, for if farmers and other laborers made barely enough money to survive, they had no extra money with which they could pay professionals like doctors and lawyers. When Atticus renders a legal service for Walter Cunningham Sr., a farmer whose property rights are in question because of an entailment, he is repaid with goods such as firewood and nuts instead of cash. This history between the two men influences events during the novel; when a lynch mob appears at the local jail, Scout recognizes Cunningham as her father's former client. The conversation she strikes up with him recalls him to his senses, and he sheepishly leads the mob away.

Symbolism

As the title of the novel implies, the mockingbird serves as an important symbol throughout the narrative. When the children receive guns for Christmas, Atticus tells them it's all right to shoot at blue jays, but "it's a sin to kill a mockingbird." As Miss Maudie Atkinson explains, it would be thoughtlessly cruel to kill innocent creatures that "don't do one thing but make music for us to enjoy." The mockingbirds are silent as Atticus takes to the street to shoot the rabid dog, and Scout describes a similar silence in the courtroom just prior to the jury pronouncing Tom Robinson guilty. The innocent but suffering mockingbird is recalled in an editorial B. B. Underwood writes about Robinson's death, and again when Scout tells her father that revealing Boo Radley's role in Bob Ewell's death would be "like shootin' a mockingbird." Another powerful symbol is contained in the snowman Scout and Jem build after Maycomb's rare snowfall. Because there is very little snow, Jem makes the base of the figure from mud; they then change their "morphodite" from black to white with a coating of snow. When Miss Maudie's house catches fire that night, the snow melts and the figure becomes black once again. Its transformation suggests that skin color is a limited distinction that reveals little about an individual's true worth.

Humor

One element of the novel's construction that shouldn't be overlooked is Lee's use of humor. The serious issues the novel grapples with are lightened by episodes that use irony and slapstick humor, among other techniques. Just prior to Bob Ewell's attack on the children, for instance, is a scene where Scout misses her cue during the Halloween pageant, only to make her entrance as a ham during Mrs. Merriweather's sober grand finale. Scout's matter-of-fact, childish recollections also provide entertainment; she recalls that when Dill ignored her, his "fiancee," in favor of Jem, "I beat him up twice but it did no good." Other characters are full of wit as well, Miss Maudie Atkinson in particular. When exasperated by Stephanie Crawford's tales of Boo Radley peeking in her windows at night, she replies, "What did you do, Stephanie, move over in the bed and make room for him?" Including such humorous portrayals of human faults enlivens a serious plot, adds depth to the characterizations, and creates a sense of familiarity and universality, all factors that have contributed to the success and popularity of the work.

Historical Context

Civil Rights in the 1950s

Despite the end of slavery almost a century before *To Kill a Mockingbird* was published in 1960 (President Abraham Lincoln issued the Emancipation Proclamation in 1863), African Americans were still denied many of their basic rights. Although Lee sets her novel in the South of the 1930s, conditions were little improved by the early 1960s in America. The Civil Rights movement was just taking shape in the 1950s, and its principles were beginning to find a voice in American courtrooms and the law. The famous 1954 U.S. Supreme Court trial of *Brown v. the Board of Education of Topeka, Kansas* declared the long-held practice of segregation in public schools unconstitutional and quickly led to desegregation of other public institutions. However, there was still considerable resistance to these changes, and many states, especially those in the South, took years before they fully integrated their schools.

Other ways blacks were demeaned by society included the segregation of public rest rooms and drinking fountains, as well as the practice of forcing blacks to ride in the back of buses. This injustice was challenged by a mild-mannered department store seamstress named Rosa Parks. After she was arrested for failing to yield her seat to a white passenger, civil rights leaders began a successful boycott of the bus system in Montgomery, Alabama, on December 5, 1955. The principal leader of the boycott was the Reverend Martin Luther King, Jr. Along with other black pastors, such as Charles K. Steele and Fred Shuttlesworth, King organized the Southern Christian Leadership Conference in January, 1957, one of the leading organizations that helped end legal segregation by the mid-1960s. The same year that Lee won a contract for the unfinished manuscript of *To Kill a Mockingbird*, Congress passed the Civil Rights Act of 1957, which provided penalties for the violation of voting rights and created the Civil Rights Commission. African Americans would not see protection and enforcement of all of their rights, however, until well into the next decade, when the Civil Rights Act of 1964, the Voting Rights Act of 1965, and the Civil Rights Bill of 1968 were passed. These laws banned racial discrimination from public places, workplaces, polling places, and housing.

Compare & Contrast

- **1930s:** During the Great Depression, unemployment rose as high as 25%; the New Deal program of government-sponsored relief leads to a deficit in the federal budget.
  1960: After a decade of record-high American production and exports,

unemployment dips to less than 5 percent, while the federal government runs a small surplus.

Today: Unemployment runs between 5 and 6 percent, while the federal government works to reduce a multi-billion dollar deficit amidst an increasingly competitive global economy.

- **1930s:** Schools are racially segregated; emphasis in the classroom was on rote learning of the basics.

1960: Although backed up by force at times, school integration laws were being enforced; the 1959 launch of the Soviet satellite *Sputnik* leads to math and science gaining increased importance.

Today: School populations are as racially diverse as their communities; classes include a focus on combining subjects and problem-solving skills.

- **1930s:** Only property owners who were white and male could serve on juries.

1960: Women and minorities could now serve on juries; while the Supreme Court ruled that eliminating jurors from duty on the basis of race is unconstitutional, many trials still exclude blacks and Hispanics.

Today: All registered voters are eligible to serve on juries, although in many cases prosecution and defense teams aim to create a jury with a racial balance favorable to their side.

- **1930s:** A big trial serves as a entertainment event for the whole town and a child who has been to the movies is unusual.

  1960: Television was becoming the dominant form of popular entertainment, while families might see films together at drive-in movie theaters.

  Today: Although television and film are still large presences, computers and computer games swiftly gain a share in the entertainment market. Trials still provide public entertainment and are featured on their own cable channel.

The justice system was similarly discriminatory in the 1950s, as blacks were excluded from juries and could be arrested, tried, and even convicted with little cause. One notable case occurred in 1955, when two white men were charged with the murder of Emmett Till, a fourteen-year-old African American youth who had allegedly harassed a white woman. Like the jury in Tom Robinson's trial, the jury for the Till case was all white and all male; the trial was also held in a segregated courtroom. Although the defense's case rested on the unlikely claims that the corpse could not be specifically identified as Till and that the defendants had been framed, the jury took only one hour to acquit the men of all charges. The men later admitted their crimes to a journalist in great detail, but were never punished for the murder.

The Great Depression and Race Relations

The events surrounding race relations in the 1950s and 1960s have a strong correspondence with those in *To Kill a Mockingbird,* which is set nearly thirty years earlier. The South, which was still steeped in its agricultural traditions, was hit hard by the Great Depression. Small farmers like Lee's Walter Cunningham Sr. often could not earn enough cash from their crops to cover their mortgages, let alone living expenses. Lee's novel captures the romanticism many white people associated with the Southern way of life, which many felt was being threatened by industrialization. Part of this tradition, however, protected such practices as sharecropping, in which tenant farmers would find themselves virtually enslaved to landowners who provided them with acreage, food, and farming supplies. The desperation sharecroppers felt was brilliantly depicted in Erskine Caldwell's 1932 novel, *Tobacco*

Road. The racism of the South—many blacks were sharecroppers—is also portrayed in Richard Wright's novel *Uncle Tom's Children* (1938).

There was little opportunity for African Americans to advance themselves in the South. Schools were segregated between whites and blacks, who were not allowed to attend white high schools. Blacks were therefore effectively denied an education, since, in the early 1930s, there was not a single high school built for black students in the South. The result was that nearly half of all blacks in the South did not have an education past the fifth grade; in *To Kill a Mockingbird,* Calpurnia tells the children she is only one of four members of her church who can read. Ironically, the Depression helped to change that when northern school boards began integrating schools to save the costs of running separate facilities. President Franklin Delano Roosevelt's New Deal also led to the creation of the National Youth Administration (founded in 1935) and its Division of Negro Affairs, which helped teach black students to read and write. The Depression was particularly painful to blacks, who, in the 1920s, were already grossly underemployed. With worsening economic times, however, they found that even the menial jobs they once had—like picking cotton—had been taken by whites. The New Deal helped here, too, with the creation of the Federal Housing Administration, the Works Progress Administration, and other agencies that assisted poor blacks in obtaining jobs and housing.

Yet the oppressive society in the South often prevented blacks from taking advantage of this government assistance. Racist groups like the Ku Klux Klan and the Black Shirts terrorized blacks out of their jobs. The vigilante practice of lynching was still common in the South in the early 1930s. Only North Carolina, South Carolina, Kentucky, and Alabama had laws specifically outlawing lynching as an illegal activity. (Surprisingly, only two northern states had similar laws.) By 1935, however, public outrage had reached a point where lynchings were no longer generally tolerated, even by whites. In Lee's novel, for instance, the local sheriff tries to warn Atticus Finch of a possible lynch mob while a concerned citizen, B. B. Underwood, is prepared to turn them away from the jail with his shotgun.

Critical Overview

Although *To Kill a Mockingbird* was a resounding popular success when it first appeared in 1960, initial critical response to Lee's novel was mixed. Some reviewers faulted the novel's climax as melodramatic, while others found the narrative point of view unbelievable. For instance, *Atlantic Monthly* contributor Phoebe Adams found Scout's narration "frankly and completely impossible, being told in the first person by a six-year-old girl with the prose style of a well-educated adult." Granville Hicks likewise observed in *Saturday Review* that "Miss Lee's problem has been to tell the story she wants to tell and yet stay within the consciousness of a child, and she hasn't consistently solved it." In contrast, Nick Aaron Ford asserted in *PHYLON* that Scout's narration "gives the most vivid, realistic, and delightful experiences of child's world ever presented by an American novelist, with the possible exception of Mark Twain's *Tom Sawyer* and *Huckleberry Finn.*"

Other early reviews of the novel focused on Lee's treatment of racial themes. Several observers remarked that while the plot of *To Kill a Mockingbird* was not particularly original, it was well executed; *New Statesman* contributor Keith Waterhouse, for instance, noted that Lee "gives freshness to a stock situation." In contrast, Harding LeMay asserted in the *New York Herald Tribune Book Review* that the author's "valiant attempt" to combine Scout's amusing recollections of her eccentric neighborhood with the serious events surrounding Tom Robinson's trial "fails to produce a novel of stature, or even of original insight," although "it does provide an exercise in easy, graceful writing." Richard Sullivan, on the other hand, claimed in the *Chicago Sunday Tribune* that *To Kill a Mockingbird* "is a novel of strong contemporary national significance. And it deserves serious consideration. But first of all it is a story so admirably done that it must be called both honorable and engrossing." The Pulitzer Prize committee agreed with this last opinion, awarding the novel its 1961 prize for fiction.

Later appraisals of the novel have also supported these favorable assessments, emphasizing the technical excellence of Lee's narration and characterizations. In a 1975 article, William T. Going called Scout's point of view "the structural *forte*" of the novel, adding that it was "misunderstood or misinterpreted" by most early critics. "Maycomb and the South, then," the critic explained, "are all seen through the eyes of Jean Louise, who speaks from the mature and witty vantage of an older woman recalling her father as well as her brother and their childhood days." Critic Fred Erisman interpreted the novel as presenting a vision for a "New South" that can retain its regional outlook and yet treat all its citizens fairly. He praised Atticus Finch as a Southern representation of the ideal man envisioned by nineteenth-century American philosopher Ralph Waldo Emerson: "the individual who vibrates to his own iron string, the one man in the town that the community trusts 'to do right,' even as they deplore his peculiarities." R. A. Dave similarly found the novel a success in its exploration of Southern history and justice. He claimed that in *To Kill a Mockingbird* "there is a complete cohesion of art and morality. And therein lies the novelist's success. She is a remarkable storyteller. The reader just glides through the novel abounding in humor and pathos, hopes and fears, love and hatred, humanity and brutality—all affording him a memorable human experience of journeying through sunshine and rain at once.... The tale of heroic struggle lingers in our memory as an unforgettable experience."

Sources

Phoebe Adams, review in *Atlantic Monthly,* Vol. 206, August 26, 1960, pp. 98-99.

R. A. Dave, *"To Kill a Mockingbird:* Harper Lee's Tragic Vision," in *Indian Studies in American Fiction,* edited by M. K. Naik, S. K. Desai, Punekar S. Mokashi, and M. Jayalakshammanni. Karnatak University Press, 1974, pp. 311-23.

Fred Erisman, "The Romantic Regionalism of Harper Lee," in *The Alabama Review,* Vol. 26, No. 2, April, 1973, pp. 122-36.

Nick Aaron Ford, review in *PHYLON,* Vol. XXII, Second Quarter (June), 1961, p. 122.

William T. Going, "Store and Mockingbird: Two Pulitzer Novels about Alabama," in his *Essays on Alabama Literature,* The University of Alabama Press, 1975, pp. 9-31.

Granville Hicks, "Three at the Outset," in *Saturday Review,* Vol. XLIII, No. 30, July 23, 1960, pp. 15-16.

Harding LeMay, "Children Play: Adults Betray," in *New York Herald Tribune Book Review,* July 10, 1960, p. 5.

Richard Sullivan, "Engrossing First Novel of Rare Excellence," *Chicago Sunday Tribune,* July 17, 1960, p. 1.

Keith Waterhouse, review in *New Statesman,*

October 15, 1960, p. 580.

For Further Study

Edwin Bruell, "Keen Scalpel on Racial Ills." *The English Journal,* Vol. 53, December, 1964, pp. 658-61.

> An article that touches on Lee's "warm" portrayal of Scout and the ironic tone in Lee's treatment of the bigoted.

Claudia Durst Johnson, *Understanding 'To Kill a Mockingbird': A Student Casebook to Issues, Sources, and Historic Documents,* Greenwood Press, 1994.

> Johnson's book is the most thorough analysis of the novel to date. She discusses the literary and historical context of the book, then analyzes its form, its connections to Gothic tradition, its treatment of prejudicial and legal boundaries, and its focus on communication. Johnson provides a large collection of sources relating to the novel, including documents about the "Scottsboro Boys" trials, the Civil Rights Movement, issues of stereotyping, the debates over Atticus in legal circles, and the censorship of the novel.

Frank H. Lyell, "One-Taxi Town," in *The New York*

Book Review, July 10, 1960, pp. 5, 18.

> Lyell praises Lee for her characterization and provides some limited criticism of her style.

Edgar H. Schuster, "Discovering Theme and Structure in the Novel," in *The English Journal,* Vol. 52, 1963, pp. 506-11.

> Schuster presents a practical classroom approach to the novel and an analysis of its themes and structure.

CPSIA information can be obtained
at www.ICGtesting.com
Printed in the USA
LVOW13s1746311017
554455LV00010B/609/P